Love

First published in English in 2015 by
Michael O'Mara Books Limited
9 Lion Yard
Tremadoc Road
London SW4 7NQ

Published in agreement with Sant Jordi Asociados Agencia Literaria S.L.U.,
Barcelona, Spain
www.santjordi-asociados.com

Text selection and editing: Márcia Botelho
Illustrations: Catalina Estrada at Folioart.co.uk
Photograph of the author: © Paul Macleod
Graphic Designer: Lene Stangebye Geving/Mercè Roig
Translation: © Margaret Jull Costa

A CIP catalogue record for this book is available from the British Library.

ISBN: 978-1-78243-490-0 in hardback print format

1 2 3 4 5 6 7 8 9 10

www.mombooks.com

Printed and bound by TBB, Slovakia

PAULO COELHO

Love

SELECTED QUOTATIONS

Michael O'Mara Books Limited

Love

Love never stops a man
from following his Personal Legend.
If that happens, it's because it isn't true Love,
the Love that speaks the Language of the World.

The Alchemist

Giving

Love is neither large nor small, it is simply love.
You cannot measure love the way you measure a road.
If you did, you would start comparing what you felt with
what other people told you or with your own hopes.
That way, you are only going to hear stories,
rather than follow your own path.

'Notes written in airports'

Risk failure, disappointment, disillusion,
but never cease in your search for love.
As long as you keep looking, you will triumph in the end.

Brida

Love is the force that transforms and improves
the Soul of the World.

The Alchemist

Everyone knows how to love,
because we are all born with that gift.
Some people have a natural talent for it,
but the majority of us have to re-learn,
to remember how to love, and everyone, without exception,
needs to burn on the bonfire of past emotions,
to relive certain joys and griefs, certain ups and downs,
until they can see the connecting thread that exists behind
each new encounter; because there is a connecting thread.

Eleven Minutes

Love is the only thing that activates our intelligence
and our creativity, that purifies and liberates us.

The Zahir

The essence of Creation is one and one alone,
and that essence is called love. Love is the force that brings
us back together, in order to condense the experience
dispersed in many lives and many parts of the world.

Brida

Love is a force that is here on earth to make us happy,
to bring us closer to God and to our fellow creatures.

The Zahir

The wise man is only wise because he loves.
The fool is only foolish because he thinks
he can understand love.

By the River Piedra I Sat Down and Wept

Love is the key
to understanding all the mysteries.

Brida

The spiritual experience is, above all,
a practical experience of love.
And in love there are no rules.
We can try to follow manuals, to control our heart,
to plan our every move, but that is all nonsense.
The heart decides, and what the heart decides
is what counts.

By the River Piedra I Sat Down and Wept

If someone is capable of loving his partner without
restrictions, unconditionally,
then he is manifesting the love of God.
If the love of God becomes manifest,
that means he loves his fellow creature too.

The Zahir

Love is the only bridge between the visible and the invisible
known to everyone. It is the only effective language
for translating the lessons that the universe teaches
to human beings every day.

Brida

Love fills everything.
It cannot be desired because it is an end in itself.
It cannot betray because it has nothing to do with
possession. It cannot be held prisoner
because it is a river and will overflow its banks.

The Witch of Portobello

There are moments when God demands obedience,
but there are also moments
when he wants to test our will
and challenge us to understand His love.

The Fifth Mountain

Love is a mysterious thing:
the more we give out, the more it grows.

'Respecting work'

Love is above everything else,
and there is no hatred in love,
only the occasional mistake.

Brida

The whole of man's life on the face of Earth can be summed
up in one thing – the search for his soulmate.
He may pretend to be running after wisdom,
money or power, but none of that matters.
Whatever he achieves will be incomplete
if he fails to find his soulmate.

Brida

Love is an act of faith in another person
and its face must always be swathed in mystery.
It should be lived and enjoyed in every moment,
but whenever we try to understand it,
the magic disappears.

'Respecting the mystery'

How does light enter a house?
Through open windows. How does light enter a person?
Through the open door of love.

Eleven Minutes

In love there is neither good nor evil,
there is neither construction nor destruction,
there is merely movement.
And love changes the laws of nature.

The Zahir

God was there in our ancestors' caves and in their
thunderstorms, and during all that time,
He never ceased to flow into man's heart in the form of love.

The Pilgrimage

When you love, you can get anything from Creation.
When you love, you have no need to understand what is
happening, because everything is happening inside
ourselves, and then men can even turn themselves
into the wind, with the wind's help.

The Alchemist

All lovers, of whichever sex,
should be warned that love, as well as being a blessing,
is also extremely dangerous, unforeseeable,
and capable of inflicting serious damage.
Consequently, anyone set on loving someone should know
that he is exposing body and soul to various kinds of
wounds, but that he cannot blame his partner,
because both run the same risks.

'Convention for those wounded in love'

In love lies the seed of our growth.
The more we love,
the closer we are to the spiritual experience.

By the River Piedra I Sat Down and Wept

Then there are those who plant.
They endure storms and all the many vicissitudes
of the seasons, and they rarely rest. But, unlike a building,
a garden never stops growing. And while it requires
the gardener's constant attention, it also allows life
for the gardener to be a great adventure.

Brida

Why should we listen to our hearts?
Because wherever your heart is,
that is where your treasure will be too.

The Alchemist

No day is the same as any other, and every morning
holds its own special miracle, its magic moment in which
old universes are destroyed and new stars created.

By the River Piedra I Sat Down and Wept

The warrior plunges unhesitatingly
into the river of passions always flowing through his life.

The Manual of the Warrior of Light

Everyone has a treasure waiting for him.

The Alchemist

The moment we set out in search of love,
love sets out to meet us – and saves us.

By the River Piedra I Sat Down and Wept

Transformation

Despite all the injustices we suffer,
despite the bad things that happen to us,
despite feeling incapable of changing
what is wrong about us and the world,
love is stronger than all of that and will help us to grow.
And only then will we be able to understand stars,
angels and miracles.

The Valkyries

God is not vengeance, God is love.
His only punishment is to oblige someone
who has interrupted a work of love to continue.

The Pilgrimage

Yes, that is love. It is what makes the hunt change
into a falcon, the falcon into a man and the man once more
into a desert. It's what makes lead change into gold,
and gold to hide itself again beneath the earth.

The Alchemist

Love is giving me a pretty hard time at the moment.
Now this could be seen as a descent
into hell or it could be seen as a revelation.

The Zahir

There is only love.
Love is what keeps the earth turning
and the stars hanging in the sky.

'Notes written in airports'

The energy of hatred won't get you anywhere;
but the energy of forgiveness,
which reveals itself through love,
will transform your life in a positive way.

The Zahir

Love can change a person.
It was through you that I discovered who I am.

The Winner Stands Alone

History will only change
when we are able to use the energy of love,
just as we use the energy of the wind,
the seas, the atom.

The Zahir

Meetings occur when we reach a limit,
when we need to die and be reborn emotionally.
These meetings are waiting for us.

Eleven Minutes

One has to keep walking the road to Santiago,
to discard any unnecessary baggage, to keep only
what you need in order to live each day,
and to allow the energy of love to flow freely,
from the outside in and from the inside out.

The Zahir

The Warrior of Light embraces his passions
and enjoys them intensely. He knows that there is no need
to renounce the pleasures of conquest; they are part of life
and bring joy to all those who participate in them,
but he never loses sight of those things that last
or of the strong bonds that are forged over time.
The warrior can distinguish between
what is transient and what will last.

The Manual of the Warrior of Light

Love is not a habit, a commitment, or a debt.
Love simply is. No definitions.
Love and don't ask too many questions.
Just love.

The Witch of Portobello

Love doesn't ask many questions,
because once we start thinking,
we start to feel afraid. It's an inexplicable fear
and there's no point putting it into words.
Risks are there to be taken.

By the River Piedra I Sat Down and Wept

People have been trying to understand
the universe through love ever
since the beginning of time.

Brida

Love isn't desire or knowledge or admiration.
It's a challenge, it's an invisible fire.

The Witch of Portobello

That's why it's so important to let certain things go.
To release them. To cut loose. People need to understand
that no one is playing with marked cards;
sometimes we win and sometimes we lose.
Don't expect to get anything back, don't expect recognition
for your efforts, don't expect your genius
to be discovered or your love to be understood.

The Zahir

Many emotions stir the human heart when it decides to set
out along the spiritual path. It could be a noble motive,
such as faith, love for one's fellow creatures or charity.

'Dialogues with the master – love is in the detail'

Your love saves me and returns me to my dreams.

By the River Piedra I Sat Down and Wept

I love you because I had a dream,
I met a king, I sold crystals, I crossed the desert,
the clans declared war, and I came to a well to ask
where an Alchemist lived. I love you because the whole
Universe conspired to help me find you.

The Alchemist

The important things always stay;
what we lose are the things we thought were important,
but which are, in fact, useless,
like the false power we use to control the energy of love.

The Zahir

Love is the only true experience of freedom,
and no one can possess anyone else.

Eleven Minutes

Duty becomes a kind of devotion,
of love unconstrained by the human condition,
and we begin to fight for what we want to happen.

'Respecting work'

For years I fought my heart,
because I was afraid of sadness, suffering, abandonment.
I always knew that true love was above all that
and that it was better to die than to stop loving.

By the River Piedra I Sat Down and Wept

Love is capable of changing a person's whole life,
from one moment to the next.

Eleven Minutes

Those wounded by love, unlike those wounded
in armed conflicts, are not victims or cruel beasts.
They chose something that is part of their life and so must
face up to the agony and ecstasy of their choice.
And those who were never wounded by love can never say
'I have lived', because they haven't.

'Convention for those wounded in love'

Never stop having doubts.
If you do, it will be because
you've stopped moving forward.

Brida

The magic moment occurs when a 'yes' or a 'no'
could change our whole life.

By the River Piedra I Sat Down and Wept

Finding one important thing in your life
doesn't mean you have to give up
all the other important things.

Brida

Overcoming

The warrior knows that he has learned something with every
battle he has fought, but many of those lessons have caused
him unnecessary suffering. More than once he has wasted his
time fighting for a lie. And he has suffered for people
who did not deserve his love.

The Manual of the Warrior of Light

In order for the true energy of love to penetrate your soul,
your soul must be as if you had just been born.
Why are people unhappy? Because they want to imprison
that energy, which is impossible.

The Zahir

Lots of people have been abandoned by the person
they most loved, and yet managed
to turn bitterness into happiness.

The Winner Stands Alone

Every human being experiences his or her own desire;
it is part of our personal treasure and although,
as an emotion, it can drive people away, generally speaking,
it brings those who are important to us closer.
It is an emotion chosen by my soul,
and it is so intense that it can infect everything
and everyone around me.

Eleven Minutes

Holy Mother of God, give me back my faith,
that I may be an instrument of Your work.
Give me the opportunity to learn through love,
because love never drove anyone from their dreams.

By the River Piedra I Sat Down and Wept

I need to write about love. I need to think and think
and write and write about love
– otherwise, my soul won't survive.

Eleven Minutes

The world will become real when man learns how to love;
until then we will live in the belief that we know what love is,
but we will always lack the courage
to confront it as it truly is.

The Zahir

True love can withstand separation.

The Witch of Portobello

A warrior of light is not afraid
of disappointments because he knows the power
of his sword and the strength of his love.

The Manual of the Warrior of Light

Being capable of a love of which I myself knew,
nothing leaves me in a state of grace.

The Zahir

All my life, I thought of love as some kind
of voluntary enslavement. Well, that's a lie: freedom only
exists when love is present. The person who gives him or
herself wholly, the person who feels most free,
is the person who loves most wholeheartedly.
And the person who loves wholeheartedly feels free.

Eleven Minutes

Be careful not to compare experiences of love.
You can't measure love the way you can the length
of a road or the height of a building.

The Witch of Portobello

Love is full of traps.
When it chooses to show itself,
it shows only its light and not the shadows
that the light can cast.

By the River Piedra I Sat Down and Wept

If you've ever felt love,
you'll know how painful it is to suffer for love.

Brida

The warrior of light tries to establish
what he can truly rely on.
And he always checks that he carries three things with him:
faith, hope and love.

The Manual of the Warrior of Light

'I'm in love and I'm afraid of suffering.'
'Don't be afraid; the only way to avoid
that suffering would be to refuse to love.'

The Zahir

Feelings – love, for example – do not grow old
along with the body. Feelings form part of a world where
there's no time, no space, no frontiers.

Brida

Love doesn't bring and never has brought happiness.
On the contrary, it's a constant state of anxiety,
a battlefield; it's sleepless nights,
asking ourselves all the time
if we're doing the right thing.
Real love is composed of ecstasy and agony.

The Witch of Portobello

Can a man extinguish the pain of loss in his heart?
No, but he can feel joy at gaining something.

The Fifth Mountain

Time is the only medicine for the wounds of love
or 'ruptures'. You have to suffer intensely and avoid all drugs,
tranquillizers and prayers to saints.

'Convention for those wounded in love'

I had to lose her in order to understand
that the taste of things recovered
is the sweetest honey we will ever know.

The Zahir

I opened a window and my heart.
The sun flooded into the room
and love flooded into my heart.

By the River Piedra I Sat Down and Wept

I could say that life has treated me unfairly
and taken from me the most important thing there is: love.
But the pain of love always passes.

The Winner Stands Alone

'Do you believe that your past loves
have taught you to love better?'
'They've taught me to know what I want.
In order to surrender myself to him,
I had to forget all the scars left by other men.'

The Zahir

Every warrior of light has hurt someone he loved.
That is why he is a warrior of light,
because he has been through all that
and yet never lost hope of being better than he is.

The Manual of the Warrior of Light

'There is no love in peace.
Anyone seeking peace through love is lost.'
She could not think of a single moment when love had
brought her peace. It had always come accompanied by
agonies, ecstasies, intense joy and profound sadness.

The Valkyries

Love gives us the strength
we need to perform impossible tasks.

'Mango T-shirts'

Courage does not mean an absence of fear,
but the ability not to let fear paralyse us.

'Hagakure and the way of the samurai'

You must be entirely in the place you choose.
A divided kingdom will not resist attacks by an adversary.

By the River Piedra I Sat Down and Wept

It is not difficult to rebuild a life.
We simply have to be aware that we continue
with the same degree of strength we had before
and know how to use that strength in our favour.

The Fifth Mountain

It is always important to know when something
has reached its end. Closing circles, shutting doors,
finishing chapters, it doesn't matter what we call it;
what matters is to leave in the past
those moments in life that are over.

The Zahir

You had to take risks,
follow some paths and abandon others.
No one can make a choice without feeling afraid.

Brida

Solidarity

Profound desire, true desire is the desire to be close to
someone. From that point onwards, things change,
the man and the woman come into play,
but what happens before – the attraction that brought
them together – is impossible to explain.
It is untouched desire in its purest state.

Eleven Minutes

We are all part of the divine spark.
We all have a purpose in creation and that purpose is called
love. Wake up to that love. What is gone cannot return.
What is about to arrive needs to be recognized.

The Winner Stands Alone

Love is a complicated path,
because it either leads us up to heaven
or hurls us down into hell.

By the River Piedra I Sat Down and Wept

Nothing else matters in this world, but love.
This was the love that Jesus felt for humanity,
and it was so great that it shook the stars
and changed the course of history.
His solitary life achieved what kings,
armies and empires could not.

The Pilgrimage

Anyone who loves in the hope
of receiving some reward is wasting his or her time.

The Devil and Miss Prym

It was normal to feel jealous,
although life had taught her that it was pointless thinking
you could own another person – anyone who believes
that is just deceiving themselves.

Eleven Minutes

When the warrior of light is tired or lonely,
he does not dream about distant men and women;
he turns to the person beside him and shares his sorrow or
his need for affection with them – with pleasure and without
guilt. A warrior knows that the farthest-flung star
in the Universe reveals itself in the things around him.

The Manual of the Warrior of Light

We all have a duty to love
and to allow love to manifest itself
in the way it thinks best.

The Witch of Portobello

Love gets lost when we start laying down rules
for when love should or shouldn't appear.

The Zahir

People give flowers as presents because flowers contain the
true meaning of love. Anyone who tries to possess a flower
will have to watch its beauty fading.
But if you simply look at a flower in a field,
you will keep it forever.

Brida

No one can possess the beautiful things of this Earth
– an afternoon of rain beating against the window
or the serenity of a sleeping child – but we can know them
and love them. It is through such moments
that God reveals himself to mankind.

Brida

People who are in love affect the environment
in which they live.

The Witch of Portobello

We are all Warriors of Light.
With the strength of our love and our will we can change
our destiny and that of many other people.

The Valkyries

True love does not consist in correcting other people's faults,
but in feeling glad when we see that things
are better than we expected.

Unpublished sayings

A Warrior of Light is in the world in order to help his fellow man and not in order to condemn his neighbour.

The Manual of the Warrior of Light

The tradition of hospitality must not die.
Whenever we welcome someone,
we open ourselves to adventure and to mystery.

'Maktub – The tradition of hospitality'

Anyone who falls in love without taking into account the common good will be condemned to live in constant fear of hurting his partner, of irritating his new love, of losing everything he built.

The Witch of Portobello

A Warrior of Light shares with others what he knows
of the path. Anyone who gives help also receives help
and needs to teach what he has learned.

The Manual of the Warrior of Light

Sometimes we try to enslave everything that we love,
as if egotism were the only way
of keeping our world in balance.

In the recesses of the heart

I prefer to accept my loneliness.
If I try to run away from it now,
I'll never find a partner again.
If I accept it, rather than fight against it,
things might change. I've noticed that loneliness gets
stronger when we try to face it down,
but gets weaker when we simply ignore it.

The Witch of Portobello

A Warrior of Light shares his world with the people he loves.
He tries to encourage them to do the things they would like
to do but for which they lack the courage.

The Manual of the Warrior of Light

Forgiveness is a two-way street:
whenever we forgive someone,
we are also forgiving ourselves.

'Stories about forgiveness'

In order to fight the Good Fight, we need help.
We need friends, and when our friends are not near,
then we have to make of loneliness our principal weapon.

The Pilgrimage

The world needs examples of people capable
of living out their dreams
and fighting for their ideas.

The Valkyries

When you love someone,
then things make even more sense.

The Alchemist

Real love is an act of total surrender.

By the River Piedra I Sat Down and Wept

Affinity

I am going to talk about love.
That has always been the aim of everything I've looked for
in my life – allowing love to manifest itself
in me without barriers, letting it fill up my blank spaces,
making me dance, smile, justify my life,
protect my son, get in touch with the heavens,
with men and women,
with all those who were placed in my path.

The Witch of Portobello

If you know Love,
then you also know the Soul of the World,
which is made up of Love.

The Alchemist

At that moment, I was behaving like a little girl
who has just found out that the world isn't full of ghosts
and curses as grown-ups have taught us. It's full of love,
regardless of how that love is manifested,
a love that forgives our mistakes and redeems our sins.

The Witch of Portobello

The farther off they are, the closer to the heart are all those
feelings that we try to repress and forget.
If we're in exile, we want to store away every tiny memory
of our roots. If we're far from the person we love,
everyone we pass in the street reminds us of them.

Eleven Minutes

The freedom of her love depended
on asking nothing and expecting nothing.

Eleven Minutes

We must look for love wherever it may be,
even if that means hours,
days and weeks of disappointment and sadness.

By the River Piedra I Sat Down and Wept

No passion is in vain, no love is ever wasted.
The energy of love can never be lost – it is more powerful
than anything else and shows itself in many ways.

The Witch of Portobello

She kept asking him what the 'meeting' was about,
and he always gave the same answer:
it's a way of recovering love.

The Zahir

There's no need to talk about love,
because love has its own voice and speaks for itself.

By the River Piedra I Sat Down and Wept

He learned things he never dreamed
he would learn: hope, fear, acceptance.

Brida

In some way which I don't understand,
joy is infectious,
as is enthusiasm and love.

The Witch of Portobello

Keeping passion at bay or surrendering blindly to it
– which of these two attitudes is the least destructive?
I don't know.

Eleven Minutes

The dunes change with the wind,
but the desert remains the same.
Our love will be like that.

The Alchemist

No one can fail to recognize the light
in the eyes of their soulmate.

Brida

Infatuation is a good thing,
it's fun and can enrich one's life greatly,
but it's not the same thing as love.
Love is beyond price and should not be exchanged
for anything.

The Valkyries

When we meet someone and fall in love,
we have a sense that the whole universe is on our side.

Eleven Minutes

There are things in life, though, which,
however we look at them, are valid for everyone.
Like love, for example.

Veronika Decides to Die

The Greeks have three words for love:
Eros, Philos and Agape.

Eros is the necessary, healthy attraction one human being
feels for another.

Philos is love in the form of friendship.
It's what I feel for you and for other people.
When the flame of Eros burns down,
it is Philos that keeps couples together.

Agape is total love, the love that devours whoever
experiences it. Anyone who knows and experiences Agape
sees that nothing else in the world matters, except loving.
This was the love that Jesus felt for humankind and it was so
great that it shook the stars and changed
the course of history.

'The other forms of love: Philos and Agape'

I'm afraid of death, but even more afraid of wasting my life.
I'm afraid of love, because it involves things that are beyond
our understanding; it sheds such a brilliant light,
but the shadow it casts frightens me.

Brida

When everything has been told
and retold countless times,
when the places I have visited,
the things I have experienced,
the steps I have taken because of her
are all transformed into distant memories,
nothing will remain but pure love.

The Zahir

True love allows each person to follow their own path,
knowing that they will never lose touch
with their soulmate.

Brida

Search

By accepting our faults and believing that we still deserve
a happy life, we will be opening a window through
which love can enter. Because anyone who is happy
can only see the world with love,
the force that regenerates everything in the Universe.

The Valkyries

It is only possible to achieve a dream
when you really want to.
Enthusiasm, passion and desire are not enough;
you need energy and concentration too.

'Hagakure and the way of the Samurai'

Today, I need to understand about pain.
It's in our daily lives, in our hidden suffering,
in the sacrifices we make.

Eleven Minutes

When desire is still in this pure state,
the man and the woman fall in love with life,
they live each moment reverently, consciously,
always ready to celebrate the next blessing.

Eleven Minutes

Love spoke to me: 'I am everything and I am nothing.
I am the wind, and I cannot enter windows
and doors that are shut.'

The Zahir

Love is always new.
It doesn't matter whether we love once,
twice or ten times in our lives,
we are always faced by an unfamiliar situation.
Love can take us up to heaven or down into hell,
but it always takes us somewhere.
We must accept it, because it feeds our very existence.

By the River Piedra I Sat Down and Wept

The Warrior of Light is a believer. Because he is sure that his
thoughts can change his life, his life begins to change.
Because he is certain that he will find love, that love appears.

The Manual of the Warrior of Light

Freedom is not the absence of commitments,
but the ability to choose – and commit myself to – what is
best for me. I continue my search for love.

The Zahir

I've discovered that the search can be as interesting
as actually finding what you're looking for.
As long as you can overcome your fear.

Brida

The Warrior of Light is constantly seeking the love
of someone, even if that means often having
to hear the word 'No', returning home defeated
and feeling rejected in body and soul.

The Manual of the Warrior of Light

I don't know if love appears suddenly,
but I know that I'm open to love, ready for love.

Brida

If I'm looking for true love,
I first have to get the mediocre loves out of my system.

Eleven Minutes

Working with enthusiasm opens up the gates to paradise,
to love that transforms
and to the choice that leads us to God.

'Twenty years on'

We only understand life
and the Universe when we find our soulmate.

Brida

Many people don't allow themselves to love
because there are a lot of things at risk,
a lot of future and a lot of past.

Veronika Decides to Die

Love does not limit us,
it widens our horizons,
so that we can see clearly what is out there
and can see even more clearly
the dark places in our hearts.

'In the recesses of the heart'

A warrior never gives in to fear when he is searching
for what he needs. Without love, he is nothing.

The Manual of the Warrior of Light

The world divides into farmers, who love the earth
and the harvest, and hunters,
who love dark forests and conquests.

The Valkyries

Love the path you are on, if you don't,
nothing makes sense.

'The manual for preserving paths'

There are no risks in love,
as you'll find out for yourself.
People have been searching for
and finding each other for thousands of years.

Brida

Every moment of searching
is a moment of finding.

The Alchemist

Those who take a new step,
but still want to maintain a little of their old life,
will end up torn to pieces by their own past.

'On changes in values'

A boat is safer when it's in port,
but that isn't what boats were built to do.

The Pilgrimage

The warrior only risks his heart for something worthwhile.

The Manual of the Warrior of Light

The art of living
with others

The art of love is like painting, it requires technique,
patience, and, above all, practice by the couple.
It requires boldness, the courage to go beyond
what people conventionally call 'making love'.

Eleven Minutes

When the warrior watches a sunset and feels no joy,
then something is wrong. At that point, he stops fighting
and goes in search of company, so that they can watch the
setting sun together. If he has difficulty in finding company,
he asks himself: 'Was I too afraid to approach someone?
Did I receive affection and not even notice?'

The Manual of the Warrior of Light

The power of love – when we love,
we want always to be better than we are.

The Alchemist

All human beings were born to love
and to live with their beloved.

The Winner Stands Alone

I know that love can only survive when it's free,
but whoever said I was anyone's slave?
I'm a slave only to my heart,
and in that case my burden is a very light one.

The Winner Stands Alone

Love is something that can be built
rather than simply discovered.

The Witch of Portobello

Anyone who is in love
is making love the whole time,
even when they're not.
When two bodies meet,
it is just the cup overflowing.

Eleven Minutes

Passion sends us signals that guide us through our lives,
and it's up to us to interpret those signs.

Eleven Minutes

In love, no one can harm anyone else;
we are each of us responsible for our own feelings
and cannot blame someone else for what we feel.

Eleven Minutes

Love stories have many things in common.
I've been through the same thing myself at some point
in my life, although I can't really remember it now.
I remember only that love came back,
in the form of a new man, new hopes, new dreams.

By the River Piedra I Sat Down and Wept

You're as capable of love as any other human being.
How did you learn? You didn't, you simply believe.
You believe, therefore you love.

The Witch of Portobello

One discovers love through the practice of love.

By the River Piedra I Sat Down and Wept

In some way which I don't understand,
joy is infectious,
as is enthusiasm and love.

The Witch of Portobello

I've always found that anyone who is loved
has more love to give.

The Witch of Portobello

In my love for a woman
I discovered love for all creatures.

The Fifth Mountain

Everyone finds their soulmate.
At some point in our lives,
we all meet our soulmate and recognize him or her.

Brida

I believe that the world would be happier
if just two people were happier.

The Zahir

After her first romantic disappointment,
she had never again given herself entirely.
She feared pain, loss and separation.
These things were inevitable on the path to love,
and the only way of avoiding them was by deciding
not to take that path at all. In order not to suffer,
you had to renounce love.

Brida

Love needs freedom in order to reveal all its charm,
even though freedom presupposes risk.

In the recesses of the heart

We all have a clock inside us, and in order to make love,
the hands on both clocks have to be pointing to the same
hour at the same time. That doesn't happen every day.
If you love another person, you don't depend
on having sex in order to feel good.

Eleven Minutes

It isn't what romantic songs tell us it is
– love simply is.

The Witch of Portobello

It's dangerous to overflow, because we might end up
flooding areas occupied by our loved ones and drowning
them with our love and enthusiasm.

Veronika Decides to Die

Let us speak about love!
Let us talk about true love, the kind that is always growing
and shaping the world and making mankind wiser.

The Pilgrimage

No one can escape his own heart.
That's why it's best to listen to what it says,
so that no blow ever takes you by surprise.

The Alchemist

Feelings should always be free.
You should never judge a future love
by what you've suffered in the past.

By the River Piedra I Sat Down and Wept

I don't regret the painful times;
I bear my scars as if they were medals.
I know that freedom has a high price,
as high as that of slavery; the only difference
is that you pay with pleasure and a smile,
even when that smile is dimmed by tears.

The Zahir

Knowing that you are capable of love is enough.

The Witch of Portobello

At every moment of our lives,
we all have one foot in a fairy tale
and the other in the abyss.

Eleven Minutes

We can allow the energy of love to flow freely,
instead of putting it in a jug
and standing it in a corner.

The Zahir

Greatness

Have pity on those who are enslaved by the silk ribbon
of love and who think they own someone,
and who feel jealous and take poison and torture themselves
because they cannot see that love changes like the wind
and like all things. But have pity, too, on those who are
scared to death of loving and reject love in the name
of a Greater Love they do not even know,
because they do not know Your law, which says:
'Whoever drinks of this water will never again be thirsty.'

The Pilgrimage

People love because they love.
There is no reason to love.

The Alchemist

The Lord never abandons someone who loves.

The Fifth Mountain

Love moves the heavens, the stars, people, flowers,
insects, and obliges us all to walk across the ice despite
the danger; it fills us with joy and with fear,
and gives meaning to everything.

The Zahir

For that is the essence of life:
the ability to love, not the name we carry around
on our passport, business card and identity card.

The Winner Stands Alone

Love justifies acts that mere human
beings cannot understand, unless they happen
to be experiencing that love themselves.

The Winner Stands Alone

If my love is real, freedom will conquer jealousy
and any pain it causes me,
since pain is also part of the natural process.

Eleven Minutes

Suffering occurs when we want other people to love us
in the way we imagine we want to be loved,
and not in the way that love should manifest itself
– free and untrammelled,
guiding us with its force and driving us on.

The Zahir

No one sacrifices
the most important thing she possesses: love.

The Witch of Portobello

Love is an untamed force.
When we try to control it, it destroys us.
When we try to imprison it, it enslaves us.
When we try to understand it,
it leaves us feeling lost and confused.

The Zahir

Perhaps love makes us old before our time
and makes us young again when youth has gone.

By the River Piedra I Sat Down and Wept

When male knowledge joins with female
transformation, then the great magical union is created,
and its name is Wisdom.

Brida

Surrendering completely to love, be it human or divine,
means giving up everything, including our own well-being
or our ability to make decisions.
It means loving in the deepest sense of the word.

The Witch of Portobello

The more you understand yourself,
the more you will understand the world.
And the closer you will be to your soulmate.

Brida

The only sin is a lack of love.
Be brave, be capable of loving, even when love seems
like a treacherous, terrible thing. Take joy in loving.
Take joy in victory. Follow what your hearts
are telling you to do.

The Valkyries

All men and all women are connected by an energy which
many people call love, but which is, in fact,
the raw material from which the Universe was built.
This energy cannot be manipulated,
it leads us gently forwards, it contains all we have to learn in
this life. If we try to make it go in the direction we want,
we end up desperate, frustrated, disillusioned,
because that energy is free and wild.

The Zahir

Love is the most important
and most vulnerable of human emotions.

Brida

She had known love before,
but until that night love had also meant fear.
That fear, however slight, was always a veil;
you could see almost everything through it,
but not the colours. And at that moment, with her Soulmate
there before her, she understood that love was a feeling
completely bound up with colour, like thousands of rainbows
superimposed one on top of the other. 'How much I missed
simply because I was afraid of missing it,' she thought.

Brida

It's easy to suffer for love of a cause or a mission;
this ennobles the heart of the person who suffers.

By the River Piedra I Sat Down and Wept

A day will come when love will be welcomed into all hearts,
and that most terrible of human experiences,
loneliness – far worse than hunger – will be banished
from the face of the Earth.

The Valkyries

When we love, we believe in something from the very depths
of our soul, in the strongest feelings that exist in the world,
and we are filled by a serenity that comes from the certainty
that nothing will destroy our faith.

The Pilgrimage

At this moment, I see only the rose.
And I thank the angel who gave me two gifts
that Christmas of 1979: the ability to open my heart
and the person best able to receive it.

'The golden rose'

We have to take risks.
We only really understand the miracle
of life when we allow the unexpected to happen.

By the River Piedra I Sat Down and Wept

Courage is the most important quality
for anyone seeking the Language of the World.

The Alchemist

Love gives us the strength to carry out
impossible tasks.

By the River Piedra I Sat Down and Wept

Anything you do can bring you close to the Supreme Wisdom, as long as you work with love in your heart.

Brida

God is love, generosity and forgiveness;
if we believe that,
we will never allow our weaknesses to paralyse us.

The Valkyries

I don't know if it's possible to love the desert,
but it is in the desert that my treasure lies hidden.

The Alchemist